A Note to Parents & Teachers—

Welcome to I See Trucks from Xist Publishing! These books are designed to inspire discovery and delight in the youngest readers. Each book features very simple sentences with visual cues to help beginners read their very first text.

You can help each child develop a lifetime love of reading right from the very start. Here are some ways to help a beginning reader get going:

- Read the book aloud as a first introduction
- Run your fingers below the words as you read each line
- Give the child the chance to finish the sentences or read repeating words while you read the rest.
- Encourage the child to read aloud every day!

Published proudly in the State of Texas, USA by Xist Publishing
www.xistpublishing.com
24200 Southwest Freeway Suite 402- 290 Rosenberg, TX 77471
All images licensed from Adobe Stock
First Edition

Hardcover ISBN: 978-1-5324-5465-3
Saddle Stitch ISBN: 978-1-5324-5559-9
Perfect Bound ISBN: 978-1-5324-5466-0
eISBN: 978-1-5324-5464-6

PUBLISHED IN TEXAS

I See Trucks
Fire Truck

written by **August Hoeft**

xist Publishing
INSPIRING DISCOVERY & DELIGHT

I see a fire truck.

The fire truck is red.

CA EXEMPT

The fire truck has a long ladder.

7.5 BAR
MAX. 110 KG.

The fire truck holds tools.

KEEP
BACK
KEEP BACK
500 FEET

The fire truck helps fight fires.

I see a fire truck.

Things to do next!

Write a Sentence

I see a _______________.

Drawing

Make a drawing of
your favorite truck.

Sharing

Talk to your classmates about
your favorite picture in this book.
Explain to them why you like it.

WORD LIST

a	is
fight	ladder
fire	long
fires	red
has	see
helps	the
holds	tools
I	truck

www.ingramcontent.com/pod-product-compliance
Ingram Content Group UK Ltd.
Pitfield, Milton Keynes, MK11 3LW, UK
UKHW022316100125
453367UK00017B/157

9 781532 454660